THE FIRST THREE ENCYCLICALS

E SUPREMI

AD DIEM ILLUM LAETISSIMUM

IUCUNDA SANE

POPE ST. PIUS X

Sainthood Press

SainthoodPress.com
Sainthood Press Edition 2017
Athens, Georgia
USA

CONTENTS

E SUPREMI

ENCYCLICAL ON THE RESTORATION OF ALL THINGS IN CHRIST

OCTOBER 4, 1903

TO THE PATRIARCHS, PRIMATES, ARCHBISHOPS, BISHOPS AND OTHER ORDINARIES IN PEACE AND COMMUNION WITH THE APOSTOLIC SEE

Venerable Brethren, Health and the Apostolic Benediction:

In addressing you for the first time from the Chair of the supreme apostolate to which We have, by the inscrutable disposition of God, been elevated, it is not necessary to remind you with what tears and warm instance We exerted Ourselves to ward off this formidable burden of the Pontificate. Unequal in merit though We be with St. Anselm, it seems to us that We may with truth make Our own the words in which he lamented when he was constrained against his will and in spite of his struggles to receive the honor of the episcopate. For to show with what dispositions of mind and will We subjected Ourselves to the most serious charge of feeding the flock of Christ, We can well adduce those same proofs of grief which he invokes in his own behalf. "My tears are witnesses," he wrote, "and the sounds and moanings issuing from the anguish of my heart, such as I never remember before to have come from me for any sorrow, before that day on which there seemed to fall upon me that great misfortune of the archbishop of Canterbury. And those who fixed their gaze on my face that day could not fail to see it . . . I, in color more like a dead than a living man, was pale for amazement and alarm. Hitherto I have resisted as far as I could, speaking the truth, my election or rather the violence done me. But now I am constrained to confess, whether I will or no, that the judgments of God oppose greater and greater resistance to my efforts, so that I see no way of escaping them. Wherefore vanquished as I am by the violence not so much of men as of God, against which there is no providing, I realize that nothing is left for me, after having prayed as much as I could and striven that this chalice should if possible pass from me without my drinking it, but to set aside my feeling and my will and resign myself entirely to the design and the will of God."

2. In truth, reasons both numerous and most weighty were not lacking to justify this resistance of Ours. For, beside the fact that We deemed Ourselves altogether unworthy through Our littleness of the honor of the Pontificate; who would not have been disturbed at seeing himself designated to succeed him who, ruling the Church with supreme wisdom for nearly

twenty-six years, showed himself adorned with such sublimity of mind, such luster of every virtue, as to attract to himself the admiration even of adversaries, and to leave his memory stamped in glorious achievements?

3. Then again, to omit other motives, We were terrified beyond all else by the disastrous state of human society today. For who can fail to see that society is, at the present time, more than in any past age, suffering from a terrible and deep-rooted malady which, developing every day and eating into its inmost being, is dragging it to destruction? You understand, Venerable Brethren, what this disease is—apostasy from God, than which in truth nothing is more allied with ruin, according to the word of the Prophet: "For behold they that go far from Thee shall perish" (Psalms 72:27). We saw therefore that, in virtue of the ministry of the Pontificate, which was to be entrusted to Us, We must hasten to find a remedy for this great evil, considering as addressed to Us that Divine command: "Lo, I have set thee this day over the nations and over kingdoms, to root up, and to pull down, and to waste, and to destroy, and to build, and to plant" (Jeremiah 1:10). But, cognizant of Our weakness, We recoiled in terror from a task as urgent as it is arduous.

4. Since, however, it has been pleasing to the Divine Will to raise Our lowliness to such sublimity of power, We take courage in Him who strengthens Us; and setting Ourselves to work, relying on the power of God, We proclaim that We have no other program in the Supreme Pontificate but that "of restoring all things in Christ" (Ephesians 1:10), so that "Christ may be all and in all" (Colossians 3:2). Some will

certainly be found who, measuring Divine things by human standards, will seek to discover secret aims of Ours, distorting them to an earthly scope and to partisan designs. To eliminate all vain delusions for such, We say to them with emphasis that We do not wish to be, and with the Divine assistance never shall be aught before human society but the Minister of God, of whose authority We are the depositary. The interests of God shall be Our interest, and for these We are resolved to spend all Our strength and Our very life. Hence, should anyone ask Us for a symbol as the expression of Our will, We will give this and no other: "To renew all things in Christ." In undertaking this glorious task, We are greatly quickened by the certainty that We shall have all of you, Venerable Brethren, as generous cooperators. Did We doubt it, We should have to regard you, unjustly, as either unconscious or heedless of that sacrilegious war which is now, almost everywhere, stirred up and fomented against God. For in truth, "The nations have raged and the peoples imagined vain things" (Psalms 2:1) against their Creator, so frequent is the cry of the enemies of God: "Depart from us" (Job 21:14). And as might be expected, we find extinguished among the majority of men all respect for the Eternal God, and no regard paid in the manifestations of public and private life to the Supreme Will—nay, every effort and every artifice is used to destroy utterly the memory and the knowledge of God.

5. When all this is considered, there is good reason to fear lest this great perversity may be as it were a foretaste, and perhaps the beginning of those evils which are reserved for the last days; and that there may be already in the world the "Son of Perdition" of whom the Apostle speaks (2 Thessalonians 2:3). Such, in truth, is the audacity and the wrath employed everywhere in persecuting religion, in combating the dogmas

of the faith, in brazen effort to uproot and destroy all relations between man and the Divinity! While, on the other hand, and this according to the same apostle is the distinguishing mark of Antichrist, man has with infinite temerity put himself in the place of God, raising himself above all that is called God; in such wise that although he cannot utterly extinguish in himself all knowledge of God, he has contemned God's majesty and, as it were, made of the universe a temple wherein he himself is to be adored. "He sitteth in the temple of God, showing himself as if he were God" (2 Thessalonians 2:2).

6. Verily, no one of sound mind can doubt the issue of this contest between man and the Most High. Man, abusing his liberty, can violate the right and the majesty of the Creator of the Universe; but the victory will ever be with God—nay, defeat is at hand at the moment when man, under the delusion of his triumph, rises up with most audacity. Of this we are assured in the holy books by God Himself. Unmindful, as it were, of His strength and greatness, He "overlooks the sins of men" (Wisdom 11:24), but swiftly, after these apparent retreats, "awaked like a mighty man that hath been surfeited with wine" (Psalms 77:65), "He shall break the heads of his enemies" (Psalms 67:22), that all may know "that God is the king of all the earth" (Psalms 66:8), "that the Gentiles may know themselves to be men" (Psalms 9:20).

7. All this, Venerable Brethren, We believe and expect with unshakable faith. But this does not prevent us also, according to the measure given to each, from exerting ourselves to hasten the work of God—and not merely by praying assiduously: "Arise, O Lord, let not man be strengthened" (Psalms 9:19), but, more important still, by affirming both by word and deed and in the light of day, God's supreme dominion over man and all things, so that His right to command and His authority may be fully realized and respected. This is imposed upon us not only as a natural duty, but by our common interest. For, Venerable Brethren, who can avoid being appalled and afflicted when he beholds, in the midst of a progress in civilization which is justly extolled, the greater part of mankind fighting among themselves so savagely as to make it seem as though strife were universal? The desire for peace is certainly harbored in every breast, and there is no one who does not ardently invoke it. But to want peace without God is an absurdity, seeing that where God is absent thence too justice flies, and when justice is taken away it is vain to cherish the hope of peace. "Peace is the work of justice" (Isaias 22:17). There are many, We are well aware, who, in their yearning for peace, that is for the tranquility of order, band themselves into societies and parties, which they style parties of order. Hope and labor lost. For there is but one party of order capable of restoring peace in the midst of all this turmoil, and that is the party of God. It is this party, therefore, that we must advance, and to it attract as many as possible, if we are really urged by the love of peace.

8. But, Venerable Brethren, we shall never, however much we exert ourselves, succeed in calling men back to the majesty and empire of God, except by means of Jesus Christ. "No one," the Apostle admonishes us, "can lay other foundation

than that which has been laid, which is Jesus Christ" (1 Corinthians 3:2). It is Christ alone "whom the Father sanctified and sent into this world" (Isaias 10:36), "the splendor of the Father and the image of His substance" (Hebrews 1:3), true God and true man: without whom nobody can know God with the knowledge for salvation, "neither doth anyone know the Father but the Son, and he to whom it shall please the Son to reveal Him" (Matthew 11:27). Hence it follows that to restore all things in Christ and to lead men back to submission to God is one and the same aim. To this, then, it behoves Us to devote Our care—to lead back mankind under the dominion of Christ; this done, We shall have brought it back to God. When We say to God We do not mean to that inert being heedless of all things human which the dream of materialists has imagined, but to the true and living God, one in nature, triple in person, Creator of the world, most wise Ordainer of all things, Lawgiver most just, who punishes the wicked and has reward in store for virtue.

9. Now the way to reach Christ is not hard to find: it is the Church. Rightly does Chrysostom inculcate: "The Church is thy hope, the Church is thy salvation, the Church is thy refuge" (*Homilia de capto Euthropio*, n. 6.). It was for this that Christ founded it, gaining it at the price of His blood, and made it the depositary of His doctrine and His laws, bestowing upon it at the same time an inexhaustible treasury of graces for the sanctification and salvation of men. You see, then, Venerable Brethren, the duty that has been imposed alike upon Us and upon you of bringing back to the discipline of the Church human society, now estranged from the wisdom of Christ; the Church will then subject it to Christ, and Christ to God. If We, through the goodness of God Himself, bring this task to a happy issue, We shall be rejoiced

to see evil giving place to good, and hear, for our gladness, "a loud voice from heaven saying: Now is come salvation, and strength, and the kingdom of our God and the power of his Christ" (Apocalypse 12:10). But if our desire to obtain this is to be fulfilled, we must use every means and exert all our energy to bring about the utter disappearance of the enormous and detestable wickedness, so characteristic of our time—the substitution of man for God; this done, it remains to restore to their ancient place of honor the most holy laws and counsels of the gospel; to proclaim aloud the truths taught by the Church, and her teachings on the sanctity of marriage, on the education and discipline of youth, on the possession and use of property, the duties that men owe to those who rule the State; and lastly to restore equilibrium between the different classes of society according to Christian precept and custom. This is what We, in submitting Ourselves to the manifestations of the Divine will, purpose to aim at during Our Pontificate, and We will use all our industry to attain it. It is for you, Venerable Brethren, to second Our efforts by your holiness, knowledge and experience and above all by your zeal for the glory of God, with no other aim than that Christ may be formed in all.

10. As to the means to be employed in attaining this great end, it seems superfluous to name them, for they are obvious of themselves. Let your first care be to form Christ in those who are destined from the duty of their vocation to form Him in others. We speak of the priests, Venerable Brethren. For all who bear the seal of the priesthood must know that they have the same mission to the people in the midst of whom they live as that which Paul proclaimed that he received in these tender words: "My little children, of whom I am in labor again until Christ be formed in you" (Galatians

4:19). But how will they be able to perform this duty if they be not first clothed with Christ themselves? And so clothed with Christ as to be able to say with the Apostle: "I live, yet not I, but Christ lives in me" (Galatians 2:20). "For me to live is Christ" (Philippians 1:21). Hence although all are included in the exhortation "to advance towards the perfect man, in the measure of the age of the fullness of Christ" (Ephesians 4:3), it is addressed before all others to those who exercise the sacerdotal ministry; thus these are called another Christ, not merely by the communication of power but by reason of the imitation of His works, and they should therefore bear stamped upon themselves the image of Christ.

11. This being so, Venerable Brethren, of what nature and magnitude is the care that must be taken by you in forming the clergy to holiness! All other tasks must yield to this one. Wherefore the chief part of your diligence will be directed to governing and ordering your seminaries aright so that they may flourish equally in the soundness of their teaching and in the spotlessness of their morals. Regard your seminary as the delight of your hearts, and neglect on its behalf none of those provisions which the Council of Trent has with admirable forethought prescribed. And when the time comes for promoting the youthful candidates to holy orders, ah! Do not forget what Paul wrote to Timothy: "Impose not hands lightly upon any man" (1 Timothy 5:22), bearing carefully in mind that as a general rule the faithful will be such as are those whom you call to the priesthood. Do not then pay heed to private interests of any kind, but have at heart only God and the Church and the eternal welfare of souls so that, as the Apostle admonishes, "you may not be partakers of the sins of others" (*Ibid.*). Then again be not lacking in solicitude for young priests who have just left the seminary. From the

bottom of Our heart, We urge you to bring them often close to your breast, which should burn with celestial fire—kindle them, inflame them, so that they may aspire solely after God and the salvation of souls. Rest assured, Venerable Brethren, that We on Our side will use the greatest diligence to prevent the members of the clergy from being drawn to the snares of a certain new and fallacious science, which savoureth not of Christ, but with masked and cunning arguments strives to open the door to the errors of rationalism and semi-rationalism; against which the Apostle warned Timothy to be on his guard, when he wrote: "Keep that which is committed to thy trust, avoiding the profane novelties of words, and oppositions of knowledge falsely so called which some promising have erred concerning the faith" (1 Timothy 6:20). This does not prevent Us from esteeming worthy of praise those young priests who dedicated themselves to useful studies in every branch of learning the better to prepare themselves to defend the truth and to refute the calumnies of the enemies of the faith. Yet We cannot conceal, nay, We proclaim in the most open manner possible that Our preference is, and ever will be, for those who, while cultivating ecclesiastical and literary erudition, dedicate themselves more closely to the welfare of souls through the exercise of those ministries proper to a priest jealous of the divine glory. "It is a great grief and a continual sorrow to our heart" (Romans 9:2) to find Jeremiah's lamentation applicable to our times: "The little ones asked for bread, and there was none to break it to them" (Lamentations 4:4). For there are not lacking among the clergy those who adapt themselves according to their bent to works of more apparent than real solidity—but not so numerous perhaps are those who, after the example of Christ, take to themselves the words of the Prophet: "The Spirit of the Lord hath anointed me, hath sent me to evangelize the poor, to heal the contrite of heart, to announce freedom to the captive, and sight to the blind" (Luke 4:18-19).

12. Yet who can fail to see, Venerable Brethren, that while men are led by reason and liberty, the principal way to restore the empire of God in their souls is religious instruction? How many there are who mimic Christ and abhor the Church and the Gospel more through ignorance than through badness of mind, of whom it may well be said: "They blaspheme whatever things they know not" (Jude 2:10). This is found to be the case not only among the people at large and among the lowest classes, who are thus easily led astray, but even among the more cultivated and among those endowed moreover with uncommon education. The result is for a great many the loss of the faith. For it is not true that the progress of knowledge extinguishes the faith; rather is it ignorance, and the more ignorance prevails the greater is the havoc wrought by incredulity. And this is why Christ commanded the Apostles: "Going forth teach all nations" (Matthew 28:19).

13. But in order that the desired fruit may be derived from this apostolate and this zeal for teaching, and that Christ may be formed in all, be it remembered, Venerable Brethren, that no means is more efficacious than charity. "For the Lord is not in the earthquake" (3 Kings 19:2)—it is vain to hope to attract souls to God by a bitter zeal. On the contrary, harm is done more often than good by taunting men harshly with their faults, and reproving their vices with asperity. True, the Apostle exhorted Timothy: "Accuse, beseech, rebuke," but he took care to add: "with all patience" (2 Timothy 4:2). Jesus has certainly left us examples of this. "Come to me," we find

Him saying, "come to me all ye that labor and are burdened and I will refresh you" (Matthew 11:28). And by those that labor and are burdened he meant only those who are slaves of sin and error. What gentleness was that shown by the Divine Master! What tenderness, what compassion towards all kinds of misery! Isaias has marvelously described His heart in the words: "I will set my spirit upon him; he shall not contend, nor cry out; the bruised reed he will not break, he will not extinguish the smoking flax" (Isaias 42:1). This charity, "patient and kind" (1 Corinthians 13:4.), will extend itself also to those who are hostile to us and persecute us. "We are reviled," thus did St. Paul protest, "and we bless; we are persecuted and we suffer it; we are blasphemed and we entreat" (1 Corinthians 4:12). They perhaps seem to be worse than they really are. Their associations with others, prejudice, the counsel, advice and example of others, and finally an ill-advised shame have dragged them to the side of the impious; but their wills are not so depraved as they themselves would seek to make people believe. Who will prevent us from hoping that the flame of Christian charity may dispel the darkness from their minds and bring to them light and the peace of God? It may be that the fruit of our labors may be slow in coming, but charity wearies not with waiting, knowing that God prepares His rewards not for the results of toil but for the good will shown in it.

14. It is true, Venerable Brethren, that in this arduous task of the restoration of the human race in Christ, neither you nor your clergy should exclude all assistance. We know that God recommended every one to have a care for his neighbor (Ecclesiasticus 17:12). For it is not priests alone, but all the faithful without exception, who must concern themselves with the interests of God and souls—not, of course,

according to their own views, but always under the direction and orders of the bishops; for to no one in the Church except you is it given to preside over, to teach, to "govern the Church of God which the Holy Ghost has placed you to rule" (Acts 20:28). Our predecessors have long since approved and blessed those Catholics who have banded together in societies of various kinds, but always religious in their aim. We, too, have no hesitation in awarding Our praise to this great idea, and We earnestly desire to see it propagated and flourish in town and country. But We wish that all such associations aim first and chiefly at the constant maintenance of Christian life, among those who belong to them. For truly it is of little avail to discuss questions with nice subtlety, or to discourse eloquently of rights and duties, when all this is unconnected with practice. The times we live in demand action—but action which consists entirely in observing with fidelity and zeal the divine laws and the precepts of the Church, in the frank and open profession of religion, in the exercise of every kind of charitable works, without regard to self interest or worldly advantage. Such luminous examples given by the great army of soldiers of Christ will be of much greater avail in moving and drawing men than words and sublime dissertations; and it will easily come about that when human respect has been driven out, and prejudices and doubting laid aside, large numbers will be won to Christ, becoming in their turn promoters of His knowledge and love which are the road to true and solid happiness. Oh! when in every city and village the law of the Lord is faithfully observed, when respect is shown for sacred things, when the Sacraments are frequented, and the ordinances of Christian life fulfilled, there will certainly be no more need for us to labor further to see all things restored in Christ. Nor is it for the attainment of eternal welfare alone that this will be of service—it will also contribute largely to temporal welfare and the advantage of human society. For when these conditions have been secured, the upper and wealthy classes will learn to be just and charitable to the lowly, and these will be able to bear with tranquility and patience the trials of a very hard lot; the citizens will obey not lust but law, reverence and love will be deemed a duty towards those that govern, "whose power comes only from God" (Romans 13:1). And then? Then, at last, it will be clear to all that the Church, such as it was instituted by Christ, must enjoy full and entire liberty and independence from all foreign dominion; and We, in demanding that same liberty, are defending not only the sacred rights of religion, but are also consulting the common weal and the safety of nations. For it continues to be true that "piety is useful for all things" (1 Timothy 4:8)—when this is strong and flourishing, "the people will" truly "sit in the fullness of peace" (Isaias 32:18).

15. May God, "who is rich in mercy" (Ephesians 2:4), benignly speed this restoration of the human race in Jesus Christ for "it is not of him that willeth, or of him that runneth, but of God that showeth mercy" (Romans 9:16). And let us, Venerable Brethren, "in the spirit of humility" (Daniel 3:39), with continuous and urgent prayer, ask this of Him through the merits of Jesus Christ. Let us turn, too, to the most powerful intercession of the Divine Mother—to obtain which We, addressing to you this Letter of Ours on the day appointed especially for commemorating the Holy Rosary, ordain and confirm all Our Predecessor's prescriptions with regard to the dedication of the present month to the august Virgin, by the public recitation of the Rosary in all churches; with the further exhortation that, as intercessors with God, appeal be also made to the most pure Spouse of Mary, the Patron of the Catholic Church, and the holy Princes of the Apostles, Peter and Paul.

16. And that all this may be realized in fulfillment of Our ardent desire, and that everything may be prosperous with you, We invoke upon you the most bountiful gifts of divine grace. And now in testimony of that most tender charity wherewith We embrace you and all the faithful whom Divine Providence has entrusted to Us, We impart with all affection in the Lord, the Apostolic Blessing to you, Venerable Brethren, to the clergy and to your people.

Given at Rome at St. Peter's, on the 4th day of October, 1903, in the first year of Our Pontificate.

PIUS X, POPE

AD DIEM ILLUM LAETISSIMUM

ENCYCLICAL ON THE IMMACULATE CONCEPTION

FEBRUARY 2, 1904

TO THE PATRIARCHS, PRIMATES, ARCHBISHOPS, BISHOPS AND OTHER ORDINARIES IN PEACE AND COMMUNION WITH THE APOSTOLIC SEE

Venerable Brethren, Health and the Apostolic Blessing:

An interval of a few months will again bring round that most happy day on which, fifty years ago, Our Predecessor Pius IX., Pontiff of holy memory, surrounded by a noble crown of Cardinals and Bishops, pronounced and promulgated with the authority of the infallible magisterium as a truth revealed by God that the Most Blessed Virgin Mary in the first instant of her conception was free from all stain of original sin. All the world knows the feelings with which the faithful of all the nations of the earth received this proclamation and the manifestations of public satisfaction and joy which greeted it, for truly there has not been in the memory of man any more universal or more harmonious expression of sentiment shown towards the august Mother of God or the Vicar of Jesus Christ.

2. And, Venerable Brethren, why should we not hope today, after the lapse of half a century, when we renew the memory of the Immaculate Virgin, that an echo of that holy joy will be awakened in our minds, and that those magnificent scenes of a distant day, of faith and of love towards the august Mother of God, will be repeated? Of all this We are, indeed, rendered ardently desirous by the devotion, united with supreme gratitude for benefits received, which We have always cherished towards the Blessed Virgin; and We have a sure pledge of the fulfillment of Our desires in the fervor of all Catholics, ready and willing as they are to multiply their testimonies of love and reverence for the great Mother of God. But We must not omit to say that this desire of Ours is especially stimulated by a sort of secret instinct which leads Us to regard as not far distant the fulfillment of those great hopes to which, certainly not rashly, the solemn promulgation of the dogma of the Immaculate Conception opened the minds of Pius, Our predecessor, and of all the Bishops of the universe.

3. Many, it is true, lament the fact that until now these hopes have been unfulfilled, and are prone to repeat the words of Jeremias: "We looked for peace and no good came; for a time of healing, and beheld fear" (Jeremias 8:15). But all such will be certainly rebuked as "men of little faith," who make no effort to penetrate the works of God or to estimate them in the light of truth. For who can number the secret gifts of grace which God has bestowed upon His Church through the intercession of the Blessed Virgin throughout this period? And even overlooking these gifts, what is to be said of the Vatican Council so opportunely convoked; or of the dogma of Papal Infallibility so suitably proclaimed to meet the errors that were about to arise; or, finally, of that new and unprecedented fervor with which the faithful of all classes and of every nation have long been flocking to venerate in person the Vicar of Christ? Surely the Providence of God has shown itself admirable in Our two predecessors, Pius and Leo, who ruled the Church in most turbulent times with such great holiness through a length of Pontificate conceded to no other before them. Then, again, no sooner had Pius IX proclaimed as a dogma of Catholic faith the exemption of Mary from the original stain, than the Virgin herself began in Lourdes those wonderful manifestations, followed by the vast and magnificent movements which have produced those two temples dedicated to the Immaculate Mother, where the prodigies which still continue to take place through her intercession furnish splendid arguments against the incredulity of our days.

4. Witnesses, then, as we are of all these great benefits which God has granted through the benign influence of the Virgin in those fifty years now about to be completed, why should we not believe that our salvation is nearer than we thought;

all the more since we know from experience that, in the dispensation of Divine Providence, when evils reach their limit, deliverance is not far distant. "Her time is near at hand, and her days shall not be prolonged. For the Lord will have mercy on Jacob and will choose one out of Israel" (Isaias 14:1). Wherefore the hope we cherish is not a vain one, that we, too, may before long repeat: "The Lord hath broken the staff of the wicked, the rod of the rulers. The whole earth is quiet and still, it is glad and hath rejoiced" (Isaias 14:5,7).

5. But the first and chief reason, Venerable Brethren, why the fiftieth anniversary of the proclamation of the dogma of the Immaculate Conception should excite a singular fervor in the souls of Christians lies for us in that restoration of all things in Christ which we have already set forth in Our first Encyclical letter. For can anyone fail to see that there is no surer or more direct road than by Mary for uniting all mankind in Christ and obtaining through Him the perfect adoption of sons, that we may be holy and immaculate in the sight of God? For if to Mary it was truly said: "Blessed art thou who hast believed because in thee shall be fulfilled the things that have been told thee by the Lord" (Luke 1:45); or in other words, that she would conceive and bring forth the Son of God and if she did receive in her breast Him who is by nature Truth itself in order that "He, generated in a new order and with a new nativity, though invisible in Himself, might become visible in our flesh" (St. Leo the Great, Serm. 2, De Nativ. Domini): the Son of God made man, being the "author and consummator of our faith"; it surely follows that His Mother most holy should be recognized as participating in the divine mysteries and as being in a manner the guardian of them, and that upon her as upon a foundation, the noblest after Christ, rises the edifice of the faith of all centuries.

6. How think otherwise? Could not God have given us, in another way than through the Virgin, the Redeemer of the human race and the Founder of the Faith? But, since Divine Providence has been pleased that we should have the Man-God through Mary, who conceived Him by the Holy Ghost and bore Him in her breast, it only remains for us to receive Christ from the hands of Mary. Hence whenever the Scriptures speak prophetically of the grace which was to appear among us, the Redeemer of mankind is almost invariably presented to us as united with His mother. The Lamb that is to rule the world will be sent—but He will be sent from the rock of the desert; the flower will blossom, but it will blossom from the root of Jesse. Adam, the father of mankind, looked to Mary crushing the serpent's head, and he dried the tears that the malediction had brought into his eyes. Noë thought of her when shut up in the ark of safety, and Abraham when prevented from the slaying of his son; Jacob at the sight of the ladder on which angels ascended and descended; Moses amazed at the sight of the bush which burned but was not consumed; David escorting the ark of God with dancing and psalmody; Elias as he looked at the little cloud that rose out of the sea. In fine, after Christ, we find in Mary the end of the law and the fulfillment of the figures and oracles.

7. And that through the Virgin, and through her more than through any other means, we have offered us a way of reaching the knowledge of Jesus Christ, cannot be doubted when it is remembered that with her alone of all others Jesus was for thirty years united, as a son is usually united with a mother, in the closest ties of intimacy and domestic life. Who

could better than His Mother have an open knowledge of the admirable mysteries of the birth and childhood of Christ, and above all of the mystery of the Incarnation, which is the beginning and the foundation of faith? Mary not only preserved and meditated on the events of Bethlehem and the facts which took place in Jerusalem in the Temple of the Lord, but sharing as she did the thoughts and the secret wishes of Christ, she may be said to have lived the very life of her Son. Hence nobody ever knew Christ so profoundly as she did, and nobody can ever be more competent as a guide and teacher of the knowledge of Christ.

8. Hence it follows, as We have already pointed out, that the Virgin is more powerful than all others as a means for uniting mankind with Christ. Hence too since, according to Christ Himself, "Now this is eternal life: That they may know thee the only truly God, and Jesus Christ whom thou hast sent" (John 17:3), and since it is through Mary that we attain to the knowledge of Christ, through Mary also we most easily obtain that life of which Christ is the source and origin.

9. And if we set ourselves to consider how many and powerful are the causes by which this most holy Mother is filled with zeal to bestow on us these precious gifts, oh, how our hopes will be expanded!

10. For is not Mary the Mother of Christ? Then she is our Mother also. And we must in truth hold that Christ, the Word made Flesh, is also the Savior of mankind. He had a physical body like that of any other man: and again as Savior of the human family, he had a spiritual and mystical body, the society, namely, of those who believe in Christ. "We are many, but one sole body in Christ" (Romans 12:5). Now the Blessed Virgin did not conceive the Eternal Son of God merely in order that He might be made man taking His human nature from her, but also in order that by means of the nature assumed from her He might be the Redeemer of men. For which reason the Angel said to the Shepherds: "Today there is born to you a Savior who is Christ the Lord" (Luke 2:11). Wherefore in the same holy bosom of his most chaste Mother, Christ took to Himself flesh, and united to Himself the spiritual body formed by those who were to believe in Him. Hence Mary, carrying the Savior within her, may be said to have also carried all those whose life was contained in the life of the Savior. Therefore all we who are united to Christ, and as the Apostle says are members of His body, of His flesh, and of His bones (Ephesians 5:30), have issued from the womb of Mary like a body united to its head. Hence, though in a spiritual and mystical fashion, we are all children of Mary, and she is Mother of us all. Mother, spiritually indeed, but truly Mother of the members of Christ, who are we (S. Aug. L. de S. Virginitate, c. 6).

11. If then the most Blessed Virgin is the Mother at once of God and men, who can doubt that she will work with all diligence to procure that Christ, Head of the Body of the Church (Colossians 1:18), may transfuse His gifts into us, His members, and above all that of knowing Him and living through Him (1 John 4:9)?

12. Moreover it was not only the prerogative of the Most Holy Mother to have furnished the material of His flesh to the Only Son of God, Who was to be born with human members (S. Bede Ven. L. Iv. in Luc. xl.), of which material should be prepared the Victim for the salvation of men; but hers was also the office of tending and nourishing that Victim, and at the appointed time presenting Him for the sacrifice. Hence that uninterrupted community of life and labors of the Son and the Mother, so that of both might have been uttered the words of the Psalmist: "My life is consumed in sorrow and my years in groans" (Psalms 30:11). When the supreme hour of the Son came, beside the Cross of Jesus there stood Mary His Mother, not merely occupied in contemplating the cruel spectacle, but rejoicing that her Only Son was offered for the salvation of mankind, and so entirely participating in His Passion, that if it had been possible she would have gladly borne all the torments that her Son bore (S. Bonav. 1. Sent d. 48, ad Litt. dub. 4). And from this community of will and suffering between Christ and Mary, she merited to become most worthily the Reparatrix of the lost world (Eadmeri Mon. De Excellentia Virg. Mariae, c. 9) and Dispensatrix of all the gifts that Our Savior purchased for us by His Death and by His Blood.

13. It cannot, of course, be denied that the dispensation of these treasures is the particular and peculiar right of Jesus Christ, for they are the exclusive fruit of His Death, who by His nature is the mediator between God and man. Nevertheless, by this companionship in sorrow and suffering already mentioned between the Mother and the Son, it has been allowed to the august Virgin to be the most powerful mediatrix and advocate of the whole world with her Divine Son (Pius IX, *Ineffabilis*). The source, then, is Jesus Christ "of

whose fullness we have all received" (John 1:16), "from whom the whole body, being compacted and fitly joined together by what every joint supplieth, according to the operation in the measure of every part, maketh increase of the body unto the edifying of itself in charity" (Ephesians 4:16). But Mary, as St. Bernard justly remarks, is the channel (Serm. de temp on the Nativ. B. V. *De Aquaeductu* n. 4); or, if you will, the connecting portion the function of which is to join the body to the head and to transmit to the body the influences and volitions of the head—We mean the neck. Yes, says St. Bernardine of Sienna, "she is the neck of Our Head, by which He communicates to His mystical body all spiritual gifts" (Quadrag. de Evangel. aetern. *Serm.* x., a. 3, c. iii.).

14. We are then, it will be seen, very far from attributing to the Mother of God a productive power of grace—a power which belongs to God alone. Yet, since Mary carries it over all in holiness and union with Jesus Christ, and has been associated by Jesus Christ in the work of redemption, she merits for us *de congruo*, in the language of theologians, what Jesus Christ merits for us *de condigno*, and she is the supreme Minister of the distribution of graces. Jesus "sitteth on the right hand of the majesty on high" (Hebrews 1:3). Mary sitteth at the right hand of her Son—a refuge so secure and a help so trusty against all dangers that we have nothing to fear or to despair of under her guidance, her patronage, her protection. (Pius IX, Bull *Ineffabilis*).

15. These principles laid down, and to return to our design, who will not see that we have with good reason claimed for Mary that—as the constant companion of Jesus from the house at Nazareth to the height of Calvary, as beyond all others initiated to the secrets of his Heart, and as the distributor, by right of her Motherhood, of the treasures of His merits—she is, for all these reasons, a most sure and efficacious assistance to us for arriving at the knowledge and love of Jesus Christ. Those, alas! furnish us by their conduct with a peremptory proof of it, who seduced by the wiles of the demon or deceived by false doctrines think they can do without the help of the Virgin. Hapless are they who neglect Mary under pretext of the honor to be paid to Jesus Christ! As if the Child could be found elsewhere than with the Mother!

16. Under these circumstances, Venerable Brethren, it is this end which all the solemnities that are everywhere being prepared in honor of the holy and Immaculate Conception of Mary should have in view. No homage is more agreeable to her, none is sweeter to her than that we should know and really love Jesus Christ. Let then crowds fill the churches—let solemn feasts be celebrated and public rejoicings be made: these are things eminently suited for enlivening our faith. But unless heart and will be added, they will all be empty forms, mere appearances of piety. At such a spectacle, the Virgin, borrowing the words of Jesus Christ, would address us with the just reproach: "This people honoureth me with their lips, but their heart is far from me" (Matthew 15:8).

17. For to be right and good, worship of the Mother of God ought to spring from the heart; acts of the body have here neither utility nor value if the acts of the soul have no part in them. Now these latter can only have one object, which is that we should fully carry out what the divine Son of Mary commands. For if true love alone has the power to unite the wills of men, it is of the first necessity that we should have one will with Mary to serve Jesus our Lord. What this most prudent Virgin said to the servants at the marriage feast of Cana, she addresses also to us: "Whatsoever he shall say to you, do ye" (John 2:5). Now here is the word of Jesus Christ: "If you would enter into life, keep the commandments" (Matthew 19:17). Let them each one fully convince himself of this, that if his piety towards the Blessed Virgin does not hinder him from sinning, or does not move his will to amend an evil life, it is a piety deceptive and lying, wanting as it is in proper effect and its natural fruit.

18. If anyone desires a confirmation of this, it may easily be found in the dogma of the Immaculate Conception of Mary. For leaving aside tradition which, as well as Scripture, is a source of truth, how has this persuasion of the Immaculate Conception of the Virgin appeared so conformed to the Catholic mind and feeling that it has been held as being one, and as it were inborn in the soul of the faithful? "We shrink from saying," is the answer of Dionysius of Chartreux, "of this woman who was to crush the head of the serpent that had been crushed by him and that Mother of God that she had ever been a daughter of the Evil One" (*Sent.* d. 3, q. 1). No, to the Christian intelligence, the idea is unthinkable that the flesh of Christ, holy, stainless, innocent, was formed in the womb of Mary of a flesh which had ever, if only for the briefest moment, contracted any stain. And why so, but

because an infinite opposition separates God from sin? There certainly we have the origin of the conviction common to all Christians that Jesus Christ, before, clothed in human nature, He cleansed us from our sins in His blood, accorded Mary the grace and special privilege of being preserved and exempted, from the first moment of her conception, from all stain of original sin.

19. If then God has such a horror of sin as to have willed to keep free the future Mother of His Son not only from stains which are voluntarily contracted but, by a special favor and in prevision of the merits of Jesus Christ, from that other stain of which the sad sign is transmitted to all us sons of Adam by a sort of hapless heritage: who can doubt that it is a duty for everyone who seeks, by his homage to gain the heart of Mary, to correct his vicious and depraved habits and to subdue the passions which incite him to evil?

20. Whoever moreover wishes, and no one ought not so to wish, that his devotion should be worthy of her and perfect, should go further and strive might and main to imitate her example. It is a divine law that those only attain everlasting happiness who have by such faithful following reproduced in themselves the form of the patience and sanctity of Jesus Christ: "for whom He foreknew, He also predestined to be made conformable to the image of His Son; that He might be the firstborn amongst many brethren" (Romans 8:29). But such generally is our infirmity that we are easily discouraged by the greatness of such an example: by the providence of God, however, another example is proposed to us, which is both as near to Christ as human nature allows, and more

nearly accords with the weakness of our nature. And this is no other than the Mother of God. "Such was Mary," very pertinently points out St. Ambrose, "that her life is an example for all." And, therefore, he rightly concludes: "Have then before your eyes, as an image, the virginity and life of Mary from whom as from a mirror shines forth the brightness of chastity and the form of virtue" (*De Virginib.* L. ii., c. ii.)

21. Now if it becomes children not to omit the imitation of any of the virtues of this most Blessed Mother, we yet wish that the faithful apply themselves by preference to the principal virtues which are, as it were, the nerves and joints of the Christian life—we mean faith, hope, and charity towards God and our neighbor. Of these virtues, the life of Mary bears in all its phases the brilliant character; but they attained their highest degree of splendor at the time when she stood by her dying Son. Jesus is nailed to the cross, and the malediction is hurled against Him that "He made Himself the Son of God" (John 19:7). But she unceasingly recognized and adored the divinity in Him. She bore His dead body to the tomb, but never for a moment doubted that He would rise again. Then the love of God with which she burned made her a partaker in the sufferings of Christ and the associate in His passion; with him moreover, as if forgetful of her own sorrow, she prayed for the pardon of the executioners although they in their hate cried out: "His blood be upon us and upon our children" (Matthew 27:25).

22. But, lest it be thought that We have lost sight of Our subject, which is the Immaculate Conception, what great and effectual succor will be found in it for the preservation and right development of those same virtues. What truly is the point of departure of the enemies of religion for the sowing of the great and serious errors by which the faith of so many is shaken? They begin by denying that man has fallen by sin and been cast down from his former position. Hence they regard as mere fables original sin and the evils that were its consequence. Humanity, vitiated in its source, vitiated in its turn the whole race of man; and thus was evil introduced amongst men and the necessity for a Redeemer involved. All this rejected it is easy to understand that no place is left for Christ, for the Church, for grace, or for anything that is above and beyond nature; in one word the whole edifice of faith is shaken from top to bottom. But let people believe and confess that the Virgin Mary has been from the first moment of her conception preserved from all stain; and it is straightway necessary that they should admit both original sin and the rehabilitation of the human race by Jesus Christ, the Gospel, and the Church, and the law of suffering. By virtue of this, Rationalism and Materialism is torn up by the roots and destroyed, and there remains to Christian wisdom the glory of having to guard and protect the truth. It is moreover a vice common to the enemies of the faith of our time especially that they repudiate and proclaim the necessity of repudiating all respect and obedience for the authority of the Church, and even of any human power, in the idea that it will thus be more easy to make an end of faith. Here we have the origin of Anarchism, than which nothing is more pernicious and pestilent to the order of things whether natural or supernatural. Now this plague, which is equally fatal to society at large and to Christianity, finds its ruin in the dogma of the Immaculate Conception, by the obligation which it imposes of recognizing in the Church a power before which

not only has the will to bow, but the intelligence to subject itself. It is from a subjection of the reason of this sort that Christian people sing thus the praise of the Mother of God: "Thou art all fair, O Mary, and the stain of original sin is not in thee" (*Mass of Immaculate Conception*). And thus, once again, is justified what the Church attributes to this august Virgin: that she has exterminated all heresies in the world.

23. And if, as the Apostle declares, faith is nothing else than the substance of things to be hoped for" (Hebrews 11:1), everyone will easily allow that our faith is confirmed and our hope aroused and strengthened by the Immaculate Conception of the Virgin. The Virgin was kept the more free from all stain of original sin because she was to be the Mother of Christ; and she was the Mother of Christ that the hope of everlasting happiness might be born again in our souls.

24. Leaving aside charity towards God, who can contemplate the Immaculate Virgin without feeling moved to fulfill that precept which Christ called peculiarly His own, namely that of loving one another as He loved us? "A great sign," thus the Apostle St. John describes a vision divinely sent him, appears in the heavens: "A woman clothed with the sun, and with the moon under her feet and a crown of twelve stars upon her head" (Apocalypse 12:1). Everyone knows that this woman signified the Virgin Mary, the stainless one who brought forth our Head. The Apostle continues: "And, being with child, she cried travailing in birth, and was in pain to be delivered" (Apocalypse 12:2). John, therefore, saw the Most Holy Mother of God already in eternal happiness, yet travailing in a

mysterious childbirth. What birth was it? Surely it was the birth of us who, still in exile, are yet to be generated to the perfect charity of God, and to eternal happiness. And the birth pains show the love and desire with which the Virgin from heaven above watches over us, and strives with unwearying prayer to bring about the fulfillment of the number of the elect.

25. This same charity we desire that all should earnestly endeavor to attain, taking special occasion from the extraordinary feasts in honor of the Immaculate Conception of the Blessed Virgin. Oh how bitterly and fiercely is Jesus Christ now being persecuted, and the most holy religion which He founded! And how grave is the peril that threatens many of being drawn away by the errors that are afoot on all sides, to the abandonment of the faith! "Then let him who thinks he stands take heed lest he fall" (1 Corinthians 10:12). And let all, with humble prayer and entreaty, implore of God, through the intercession of Mary, that those who have abandoned the truth may repent. We know, indeed, from experience that such prayer, born of charity and relying on the Virgin, has never been vain. True, even in the future, the strife against the Church will never cease, "for there must be also heresies, that they also who are reproved may be made manifest among you" (1 Corinthians 11:19). But neither will the Virgin ever cease to succor us in our trials, however grave they be, and to carry on the fight fought by her since her conception, so that every day we may repeat: "Today the head of the serpent of old was crushed by her" (Office Immac. Con., 11. *Vespers, Magnif.*).

26. And that heavenly graces may help Us more abundantly than usual during this year in which We pay her fuller honor, to attain the imitation of the Virgin, and that thus We may more easily secure Our object of restoring all things in Christ, We have determined, after the example of Our Predecessors at the beginning of their Pontificates, to grant to the Catholic world an extraordinary indulgence in the form of a Jubilee.

27. Wherefore, confiding in the mercy of Almighty God and in the authority of the Blessed Apostles Peter and Paul, by virtue of that power of binding and loosing which, unworthy though We are, the Lord has given Us, We do concede and impart the most plenary indulgence of all their sins to the faithful, all and several of both sexes, dwelling in this Our beloved City, or coming into it, who from the first Sunday in Lent, that is from the 21st of February, to the second day of June, the solemnity of the Most Sacred Body of Christ, inclusively, shall three times visit one of the four Patriarchal basilicas, and there for some time pray God for the liberty and exaltation of the Catholic Church and this Apostolic See, for the extirpation of heresies and the conversion of all who are in error, for the concord of Christian Princes and the peace and unity of all the faithful, and according to Our intention; and who, within the said period, shall fast once, using only meager fare, excepting the days not included in the Lenten Indult; and, after confessing their sins, shall receive the most holy Sacrament of the Eucharist; and to all others, wherever they be, dwelling outside this city, who, within the time above mentioned or during a space of three months, even not continuous, to be definitely appointed by the ordinaries according to the convenience of the faithful, but before the eighth day of December, shall three times visit the cathedral church, if there be one, or, if not, the parish church;

or, in the absence of this, the principal church; and shall devoutly fulfill the other works abovementioned. And We do at the same time permit that this indulgence, which is to be gained only once, may be applied in suffrage for the souls which have passed from this life united in charity with God.

28. We do, moreover, concede that travelers by land or sea may gain the same indulgence immediately when they return to their homes, provided they perform the works already noted.

29. To confessors approved by their respective ordinaries, We grant faculties for commuting the above works enjoined by Us for other works of piety, and this concession shall be applicable not only to regulars of both sexes, but to all others who cannot perform the works prescribed, and We do grant faculties also to dispense from Communion children who have not yet been admitted to it.

30. Moreover to the faithful, all and several, the laity and the clergy both secular and regular of all orders and institutes, even those calling for special mention, We do grant permission and power, for this sole object, to select any priest regular or secular, among those actually approved (which faculty may also be used by nuns, novices and other women living in the cloister, provided the confessor they select be one approved for nuns) by whom, when they have confessed to him within the prescribed time with the intention of gaining the present jubilee and of fulfilling all the other works

requisite for gaining it, they may on this sole occasion, and only in the forum of conscience, be absolved from all excommunication, suspension and every other ecclesiastical sentence and censure pronounced or inflicted for any cause by the law or by a judge, including those reserved to the ordinary and to Us, or to the Apostolic See, even in cases reserved in a special manner to anybody whomsoever and to Us and to the Apostolic See; and they may also be absolved from all sin or excess, even those reserved to the ordinaries themselves and to Us and to the Apostolic See, on condition however that a salutary penance be enjoined together with the other prescriptions of the law, and in the case of heresy, after the abjuration and retraction of error as is enjoined by the law; and the said priests may further commute to other pious and salutary works all vows even those taken under oath and reserved to the Apostolic See (except those of chastity, of religion, and of obligations which have been accepted by a third person); and with the said penitents, even regulars, in sacred orders such confessions may dispense from all secret irregularities contracted solely by violation of censures affecting the exercise of said orders and promotion to higher orders.

31. But We do not intend by the present Letters to dispense from any irregularities whatsoever, or from crime or defect, public or private, contracted in any manner through notoriety or other incapacity or inability; nor do We intend to derogate from the Constitution with its accompanying declaration, published by Benedict XIV, of happy memory, which begins with the words *Sacramentum poenitentiae*; nor is it Our intention that these present Letters may, or can, in any way, avail those who, by Us and the Apostolic See, or by any ecclesiastical judge, have been by name excommunicated, suspended,

interdicted or declared under other sentences or censures, or who have been publicly denounced, unless they do within the allotted time satisfy, or, when necessary, come to an arrangement with the parties concerned.

32. To all this We are pleased to add that We do concede and will that all retain during this time of Jubilee the privilege of gaining all other indulgences, not excepting plenary indulgences, which have been granted by Our Predecessors or by Ourself.

33. We close these letters, Venerable Brethren, by manifesting anew the great hope We earnestly cherish that, through this extraordinary gift of Jubilee granted by Us under the auspices of the Immaculate Virgin, large numbers of those who are unhappily separated from Jesus Christ may return to Him, and that love of virtue and fervor of devotion may flourish anew among the Christian people. Fifty years ago, when Pius IX proclaimed as an article of faith the Immaculate Conception of the most Blessed Mother of Christ, it seemed, as we have already said, as if an incredible wealth of grace were poured out upon the earth; and with the increase of confidence in the Virgin Mother of God, the old religious spirit of the people was everywhere greatly augmented. Is it forbidden us to hope for still greater things for the future? True, we are passing through disastrous times, when we may well make our own the lamentation of the Prophet: "There is no truth and no mercy and no knowledge of God on the earth. Blasphemy and lying and homicide and theft and adultery have inundated it" (Osee 4:1-2). Yet in the midst of this deluge of evil, the Virgin Most Clement rises before our

eyes like a rainbow, as the arbiter of peace between God and man: "I will set my bow in the clouds and it shall be the sign of a covenant between me and between the earth" (Genesis 9:13). Let the storm rage and sky darken—not for that shall we be dismayed. "And the bow shall be in the clouds, and I shall see it and shall remember the everlasting covenant" (*Ibid.* 16). "And there shall no more be waters of a flood to destroy all flesh" (*Ibid.* 15.). Oh yes, if we trust as we should in Mary, now especially when we are about to celebrate, with more than usual fervor, her Immaculate Conception, we shall recognize in her that Virgin most powerful, "who with virginal foot did crush the head of the serpent" (Off. Immac. Conc.).

34. In pledge of these graces, Venerable Brethren, We impart the Apostolic Benediction lovingly in the Lord to you and to your people.

Given at Rome in St. Peter's on the second day of February, 1904, in the first year of Our Pontificate.

PIUS X, POPE

IUCUNDA SANE

ENCYCLICAL ON POPE GREGORY THE GREAT

MARCH 12, 1904

TO OUR VENERABLE BRETHREN, THE PATRIARCHS, PRIMATES, ARCHBISHOPS, BISHOPS AND OTHER ORDINARIES IN PEACE AND COMMUNION WITH THE APOSTOLIC SEE

Venerable Brethren, Health and the Apostolic Benediction:

1. Joyful indeed comes the remembrance, Venerable Brethren, of that great and incomparable man, the Pontiff Gregory, first of the name, whose centenary solemnity, at the close of the thirteenth century since his death, we are about to celebrate. By that God who killeth and maketh alive, who humbleth and exalteth, it was ordained, not, We think, without a special providence, that amid the almost

innumerable cares of Our Apostolic ministry, amid all the anxieties which the government of the Universal Church imposes upon Us, amid our pressing solicitude to satisfy as best We may your claims, Venerable Brethren, who have been called to a share in Our Apostolate, and those of all the faithful entrusted to Our care, Our gaze at the beginning of Our Pontificate should be turned at once towards that most holy and illustrious Predecessor of Ours, the honor of the Church and its glory. For Our heart is filled with great confidence in his most powerful intercession with God, and strengthened by the memory of the sublime maxims he inculcated in his lofty office and of the virtues devoutly practiced by him. And since by the force of the former and the fruitfulness of the latter he has left on God's Church a mark so vast, so deep, so lasting, that his contemporaries and posterity have justly given him the name of Great, and today, after all these centuries, the eulogy of his epitaph is still verified: "He lives eternal in every place by his innumerable good works" (Apud Joann. Diac., *Vita Greg.* iv. 68), it will surely be given, with the help of Divine grace, to all followers of his wonderful example, to fulfill the duties of their own offices, as far as human weakness permits.

2. There is but little need to repeat here what public documents have made known to all. When Gregory assumed the Supreme Pontificate, the disorder in public affairs had reached its climax; the ancient civilization had all but disappeared and barbarism was spreading throughout the dominions of the crumbling Roman Empire. Italy, abandoned by the Emperors of Byzantium, had been left a prey of the still unsettled Lombards, who roamed up and down the whole country laying waste everywhere with fire and sword and bringing desolation and death in their train.

This very city, threatened from without by its enemies, tried from within by the scourges of pestilence, floods and famine, was reduced to such a miserable plight that it had become a problem how to keep the breath of life in the citizens and in the immense multitudes who flocked hither for refuge. Here were to be found men and women of all conditions, bishops and priests carrying the sacred vessels they had saved from plunder, monks and innocent spouses of Christ who had sought safety in flight from the swords of the enemy or from the brutal insults of abandoned men. Gregory himself calls the Church of Rome: "An old ship woefully shattered; for the waters are entering on all sides, and the joints, buffeted by the daily stress of the storm, are growing rotten and herald shipwreck" (*Registrum* i., 4 ad Joannem episcop. Constantino.). But the pilot raised up by God had a strong hand, and when placed at the helm, succeeding not only in making the port in despite of the raging seas, but in saving the vessel from future storms.

3. Truly wonderful is the work he was able to effect during his reign of little more than thirteen years. He was the restorer of Christian life in its entirety, stimulating the devotion of the faithful, the observance of the monks, the discipline of the clergy, the pastoral solicitude of the bishops. *Most prudent father of the family of Christ* that he was (Joann. Diac., *Vita Greg.* ii. 51), he preserved and increased the patrimony of the Church, and liberally succored the impoverished people, Christian society, and individual churches, according to the necessities of each. *Becoming truly God's Consul* (Epitaph), he pushed his fruitful activity far beyond the walls of Rome, and entirely for the advantage of civilized society. He opposed energetically the unjust claims of the Byzantine Emperors; he checked the audacity and

curbed the shameless avarice of the exarchs and the imperial administrators, and stood up in public as the defender of social justice. He tamed the ferocity of the Lombards, and did not hesitate to meet Agulfus at the gates of Rome in order to prevail upon him to raise the siege of the city, just as the Pontiff Leo the Great did in the case of Attila; nor did he desist in his prayers, in his gentle persuasion, in his skillful negotiation, until he saw that dreaded people settle down and adopt a more regular government; until he knew that they were won to the Catholic faith, mainly through the influence of the pious Queen Theodolinda, his daughter in Christ. Hence Gregory may justly be called the savior and liberator of Italy—*his own land,* as he tenderly calls her.

4. Through his incessant pastoral care, the embers of heresy in Italy and Africa die out, ecclesiastical life in the Gauls is reorganized, the Visigoths of the Spains are welded together in the conversion which has already been begun among them, and the renowned English nation, which, "situated in a corner of the world, while it had hitherto remained obstinate in the worship of wood and stone" (*Reg.* viii. 29, 30, ad Eulog. Episcop. Alexandr.), now also receives the true faith of Christ. Gregory's heart overflowed with joy at the news of this precious conquest, for his is the heart of a father embracing his most beloved son, and in attributing all the merit of it to Jesus the Redeemer, "for whose love," as he himself writes, "we are seeking our unknown brethren in Britain, and through whose grace we find unknown ones we were seeking" (*Reg.* xi. 36 (28), ad Augustin. Anglorum Episcopum). And so grateful to the Holy Pontiff was the English nation that they called him always: *our Master, our Doctor, our Apostle, our Pope, our Gregory,* and considered itself as the seal of his apostolate. In fine, so salutary and so

efficacious was his action that the memory of the works wrought by him became deeply impressed on the minds of posterity, especially during the Middle Ages, which breathed, so to say, the atmosphere infused by him, fed on his words, conformed its life and manners according to the example inculcated by him, with the result that Christian social civilization was happily introduced into the world in opposition to the Roman civilization of the preceding centuries, which now passed away for ever.

5. *This is the change of the right hand of the Most High!* And well may it be said that in the mind of Gregory the hand of God alone was operative in these great events. What he wrote to the most holy monk Augustine about this same conversion of the English may be equally applied to all the rest of his apostolic action: "Whose work is this but His who said: My Father worketh till now, and I work? (John 5:17). To show the world that He wished to convert it, not by the wisdom of men, but by His own power, He chose unlettered men to be preachers to the world; and the same He has now done, vouchsafing to accomplish through weak men great things among the nation of the Angles" (*Reg.* xi. 36 (28)). We, indeed, may discern much that the holy Pontiff's profound humility hid from his own sight: his knowledge of affairs, his talent for bringing his undertakings to a successful issue, the wonderful prudence shown in all his provisions, his assiduous vigilance, his persevering solicitude. But it is, nevertheless, true that he never put himself forward as one invested with the might and power of the great ones of the earth, for instead of using the exalted prestige of the Pontifical dignity, he preferred to call himself the *Servant of the Servants of God*, a title which he was the first to adopt. It was not merely by profane science or the "persuasive words of human wisdom"

(1 Corinthians 2:4) that he traced out his career, or by the devices of civil politics, or by systems of social renovation, skillfully studied, prepared and put in execution; nor yet, and this is very striking, by setting before himself a vast program of apostolic action to be gradually realized; for we know that, on the contrary, his mind was full of the idea of the approaching end of the world, which was to have left him but little time for great exploits. Very delicate and fragile of body though he was, and constantly afflicted by infirmities which several times brought him to the point of death, he yet possessed an incredible energy of soul which was for ever receiving fresh vigor from his lively faith in the infallible words of Christ, and in His Divine promises. Then again, he counted with unlimited confidence on the supernatural force given by God to the Church for the successful accomplishment of her divine mission in the world. The constant aim of his life, as shown in all his words and works, was, therefore, this: to preserve in himself, and to stimulate in others, this same lively faith and confidence, doing all the good possible at the moment in expectation of the Divine judgment.

6. And this produced in him the fixed resolve to adopt for the salvation of all the abundant wealth of supernatural means given by God to His Church, such as the infallible teaching of revealed truth, and the preaching of the same teaching in the whole world, and the sacraments which have the power of infusing or increasing the life of the soul, and the grace of prayer in the name of Christ, which assures heavenly protection.

7. These memories, Venerable Brethren, are a source of unspeakable comfort to Us. When We glance around from the walls of the Vatican, We find that like Gregory, and perhaps with even more reason than he, We have grounds for fear, with so many storms gathering on every side, with so many hostile forces massed and advancing against Us, and at the same time so utterly deprived are We of all human aid to ward off the former and to help us to meet the shock of the latter. But when We consider the place on which Our feet rest and on which this Pontifical See is rooted, We feel Ourself perfectly safe on the rock of Holy Church. "For who does not know," wrote St. Gregory to the Patriarch Eulogius of Alexandria, "that Holy Church stands on the solidity of the Prince of the Apostles, who got his name from his firmness, for he was called Peter from the word rock?" (*Registr.* vii. 37 (40)). Supernatural force has never, during the flight of ages, been found wanting in the Church, nor have Christ's promises failed; these remain today just as they were when they brought consolation to Gregory's heart—nay, they are endowed with even greater force for Us after having stood the test of centuries and so many changes of circumstances and events.

8. Kingdoms and empires have passed away; peoples once renowned for their history and civilization have disappeared; time and again the nations, as though overwhelmed by the weight of years, have fallen asunder; while the Church, indefectible in her essence, united by ties indissoluble with her heavenly Spouse, is here today radiant with eternal youth, strong with the same primitive vigor with which she came from the Heart of Christ dead upon the Cross. Men powerful in the world have risen up against her. They have disappeared, and she remains. Philosophical systems without

number, of every form and every kind, rose up against her, arrogantly vaunting themselves her masters, as though they had at last destroyed the doctrine of the Church, refuted the dogmas of her faith, proved the absurdity of her teachings. But those systems, one after another, have passed into books of history, forgotten, bankrupt; while from the Rock of Peter, the light of truth shines forth as brilliantly as on the day when Jesus first kindled it on His appearance in the world, and fed it with His Divine words: "Heaven and earth shall pass, but my words shall not pass" (Matthew 24:35).

9. We, strengthened by this faith, firmly established on this rock, realizing to the full all the heavy duties that the Primacy imposes on Us—but also all the vigor that comes to Us from the Divine Will—calmly wait until all the voices be scattered to the winds that now shout around Us proclaiming that the Church has gone beyond her time, that her doctrines are passed away for ever, that the day is at hand when she will be condemned either to accept the tenets of a godless science and civilization or to disappear from human society. Yet, at the same time, We cannot but remind all, great and small, as Pope St. Gregory did, of the absolute necessity of having recourse to this Church in order to have eternal salvation, to follow the right road of reason, to feed on the truth, to obtain peace and even happiness in this life.

10. Wherefore, to use the words of the Holy Pontiff, "Turn your steps towards this unshaken rock upon which Our Savior founded the Universal Church, so that the path of him who is sincere of heart may not be lost in devious windings" (*Reg.* viii. 24, ad Sabin. episcop.). It is only the charity of the

Church and union with her which "unite what is divided, restore order where there is confusion, temper inequalities, fill up imperfections" (*Registr.* v. 58 (53) ad Virgil. episcop.). It is to be firmly held "that nobody can rightly govern in earthly things, unless he knows how to treat divine things, and that the peace of States depends upon the universal peace of the Church" (*Registr.* v. 37 (20) ad Mauric. Aug.). Hence the absolute necessity of a perfect harmony between the two powers, ecclesiastical and civil, each being by the will of God called to sustain the other. For, "power over all men was given from heaven, that those who aspire to do well may be aided, that the path to heaven may be made broader, and that earthly sovereignty may be handmaid to heavenly sovereignty" (*Registr.* iii. 61 (65) ad Mauric. Aug.).

11. From these principles was derived that unconquerable firmness shown by Gregory, which We, with the help of God, will study to imitate, resolved to defend at all costs the rights and prerogatives of which the Roman Pontificate is the guardian and the defender before God and man. But it was the same Gregory who wrote to the patriarchs of Alexandria and Antioch: When the rights of the Church are in question, "we must show, even by our death, that we do not, through love of some private interest of our own want anything contrary to the common weal" (*Registr.* v. 41). And to the Emperor Maurice: "He who through vainglory raises his neck against God Almighty and against the statutes of the Fathers, shall not bend my neck to him, not even with the cutting of swords, as I trust in the same God Almighty" (*Registr.* v. 37). And to the Deacon Sabinian: "I am ready to die rather than permit that the Church degenerate in my days. And you know well my ways, that I am longsuffering; but when I decide not

to bear any longer, I face danger with a joyful soul" (*Registr.* v. 6 (iv. 47)).

12. Such were the fundamental maxims which the Pontiff Gregory constantly proclaimed, and men listened to him. And thus, with Princes and peoples docile to his words, the world regained true salvation, and put itself on the path of a civilization which was noble and fruitful in blessings in proportion as it was founded on the incontrovertible dictates of reason and moral discipline, and derived its force from truth divinely revealed and from the maxims of the Gospel.

13. But in those days the people, albeit rude, ignorant, and still destitute of all civilization, were eager for life, and this no one could give except Christ, through the Church, who "came that they may have life and have it more abundantly" (John 10:10). And truly they had life and had it abundantly, precisely because, as no other life but the supernatural life of souls could come from the Church, this includes in itself and gives additional vigor to all the energies of life, even in the natural order. "If the root be holy so are the branches," said St. Paul to the Gentiles, "and thou being a wild olive art ingrafted in them, and art made partaker of the root and of the fatness of the olive tree" (Romans 11:16, 17).

14. Today, on the contrary, although the world enjoys a light so full of Christian civilization, and in this respect cannot for a moment be compared with the times of Gregory, yet it seems as though it were tired of that life, which has been, and

still is, the chief and often the sole fount of so many blessings—and not merely past but present blessings. And not only does this useless branch cut itself off from the trunk, as happened in other times when heresies and schisms arose, but it first lays the ax to the root of the tree, which is the Church, and strives to dry up its vital sap that its ruin may be the surer and that it may never blossom again.

15. In this error, which is the chief one of our time and the source whence all the others spring, lies the origin of so much loss of eternal salvation among men, and of all the ruins affecting religion which we continue to lament, and of the many others which we still fear will happen if the evil be not remedied. For all supernatural order is denied, and, as a consequence, the divine intervention in the order of creation and in the government of the world and in the possibility of miracles; and when all these are taken away, the foundations of the Christian religion are necessarily shaken. Men even go so far as to impugn the arguments for the existence of God, denying with unparalleled audacity and against the first principles of reason the invincible force of the proof, which from the effects ascends to their cause, that is God, and to the notion of His infinite attributes. "For the invisible things of him, from the creation of the world, are clearly seen, being understood by the things that are made: his eternal power also and divinity" (Romans 1:20). The way is thus opened to other most grievous errors, equally repugnant to right reason and pernicious to good morals.

16. The gratuitous negation of the supernatural principles, proper to *knowledge falsely so called*, has actually become the postulate of a historical criticism equally false. Everything that relates in any way to the supernatural order, either as belonging to it, constituting it, presupposing it, or merely finding its explanation in it, is erased without further investigation from the pages of history. Such are the Divinity of Jesus Christ, His Incarnation through the operation of the Holy Ghost, His Resurrection by His own power, and in general all the dogmas of our faith. Science once placed on this false road, there is no law of criticism to hold it back; and it cancels at its own caprice from the holy books everything that does not suit it or that it believes to be opposed to the pre-established theses it wishes to demonstrate. For take away the supernatural order and the story of the origin of the Church must be built on quite another foundation, and hence the innovators handle as they list the monuments of history, forcing them to say what they wish them to say, and not what the authors of those monuments meant.

17. Many are captivated by the great show of erudition which is held out before them, and by the apparently convincing force of the proofs adduced, so that they either lose the faith or feel that it is greatly shaken in them. There are many, too, firm in the faith, who accuse critical science of being destructive, while in itself it is innocent and a sure element of investigation when rightly applied. Both the former and the latter fail to see that they start from a false hypothesis, that is to say, from science falsely so-called, which logically forces them to conclusions equally false. For given a false philosophical principle, everything deduced from it is vitiated. But these errors will never be effectively refuted unless, by bringing about a change of front, that is to say, unless those

in error be forced to leave the field of criticism in which they consider themselves firmly entrenched for the legitimate field of philosophy, through the abandonment of which they have fallen into their errors.

18. Meanwhile, however, it is painful to have to apply to men not lacking in acumen and application the rebuke addressed by St. Paul to those who fail to rise from earthly things to the things that are invisible: "They became vain in their thoughts and their foolish heart was darkened; for professing themselves to be wise they became fools" (Romans 1:21, 22). And surely foolish is the only name for him who consumes all his intellectual forces in building upon sand.

19. Not less deplorable are the injuries which accrue from this negation to the moral life of individuals and of civil society. Take away the principle that there is anything divine outside this visible world, and you take away all check upon unbridled passions even of the lowest and most shameful kind, and the minds that become slaves to them riot in disorders of every species. "God gave them up to the desires of their heart, unto uncleanness, to dishonor their own bodies among themselves" (Romans 1:24). You are well aware, Venerable Brethren, how truly the plague of depravity triumphs on all sides, and how the civil authority, wherever it fails to have recourse to the means of help offered by the supernatural order, finds itself quite unequal to the task of checking it. Nay, authority will never be able to heal other evils as long as it forgets or denies that all power comes from God. The only check a government can command in this case is that of force; but force cannot be constantly employed, nor is it

always available, yet the people continue to be undermined as by a secret disease, they become discontented with everything, they proclaim the right to act as they please, they stir up rebellions, they provoke revolutions, often of extreme violence, in the State; they overthrow all rights human and divine. Take away God, and all respect for civil laws, all regard for even the most necessary institutions, disappears; justice is scouted; the very liberty that belongs to the law of nature is trodden underfoot; and men go so far as to destroy the very structure of the family, which is the first and firmest foundation of the social structure. The result is that in these days hostile to Christ, it has become more difficult to apply the powerful remedies which the Redeemer has put into the hands of the Church in order to keep the peoples within the lines of duty.

20. Yet there is no salvation for the world but in Christ: "For there is no other name under heaven given to men whereby we may be saved" (Acts 4:12). To Christ then we must return. At His feet we must prostrate ourselves to hear from His divine mouth the words of eternal life, for He alone can show us the way of regeneration, He alone teach us the truth, He alone restore life to us. It is He who has said: "I am the way, the truth, and the life" (John 14:16). Men have once more attempted to work here below without Him, they have begun to build up the edifice after rejecting the corner stone, as the Apostle Peter rebuked the executioners of Jesus for doing. And lo! The pile that has been raised again crumbles and falls upon the heads of the builders, crushing them. But Jesus remains for ever the corner stone of human society, and again the truth becomes apparent that without Him there is no salvation: "This is the stone which has been rejected by you,

the builders, and which has become the head of the corner, neither is there salvation in any other" (Acts 4:11, 12).

21. From all this you will easily see, Venerable Brethren, the absolute necessity imposed upon every one of us to receive with all the energy of our souls and with all the means at our disposal, this supernatural life in every branch of society—in the poor working man who earns his morsel of bread by the sweat of his brow, from morning to night, and in the great ones of the earth who preside over the destiny of nations. We must, above all else, have recourse to prayer, both public and private, to implore the mercies of the Lord and His powerful assistance. "Lord, save us—we perish" (Matthew 8:25), we must repeat like the Apostles when buffeted by the storm.

22. But this is not enough. Gregory rebukes the bishop who, through love of spiritual solitude and prayer, fails to go out into the battlefield to combat strenuously for the cause of the Lord: "The name of bishop, which he bears, is an empty one." And rightly so, for men's intellects are to be enlightened by continual preaching of the truth, and errors are to be efficaciously refuted by the principles of true and solid philosophy and theology, and by all the means provided by the genuine progress of historical investigation. It is still more necessary to inculcate properly on the minds of all the moral maxims taught by Jesus Christ, so that everybody may learn to conquer himself, to curb the passions of the mind, to stifle pride, to live in obedience to authority, to love justice, to show charity towards all, to temper with Christian love the bitterness of social inequalities, to detach the heart from the goods of the world, to live contented with the state in which

Providence has placed us, while striving to better it by the fulfillment of our duties, to thirst after the future life in the hope of eternal reward. But, above all, is it necessary that these principles be instilled and made to penetrate into the heart, so that true and solid piety may strike root there, and all, both as men and as Christians, may recognize by their acts, as well as by their words, the duties of their state and have recourse with filial confidence to the Church and her ministers to obtain from them pardon for their sins, to receive the strengthening grace of the Sacraments, and to regulate their lives according to the laws of Christianity.

23. With these chief duties of the spiritual ministry, it is necessary to unite the charity of Christ, and when this moves us there will be nobody in affliction who will not be consoled by us, no tears that will not be dried by our hands, no need that will not be relieved by us. To the exercise of this charity let us dedicate ourselves wholly; let all our own affairs give way before it, let our personal interests and convenience be set aside for it, making ourselves "all things to all men" (1 Corinthians 9:22), to gain all men to the Lord, giving up our very life itself, after the example of Christ: "The good shepherd gives his life for his sheep" (John 10:11).

24. These precious admonitions abound in the pages which the Pontiff St. Gregory has left written, and they are expressed with far greater force in the manifold examples of his admirable life.

25. Now, since all this springs necessarily both from the nature of the principles of Christian revelation, and from the intrinsic properties which Our Apostolate should have, you see clearly, Venerable Brethren, how mistaken are those who think they are doing service to the Church, and producing fruit for the salvation of souls, when by a kind of prudence of the flesh they show themselves liberal in concessions to science falsely so-called, under the fatal illusion that they are thus able more easily to win over those in error, but really with the continual danger of being themselves lost. The truth is one, and it cannot be halved; it lasts forever, and is not subject to the vicissitudes of the times. "Jesus Christ, today and yesterday, and the same for ever" (Hebrews 13:8).

26. And so, too, are all they seriously mistaken who, occupying themselves with the welfare of the people, and especially upholding the cause of the lower classes, seek to promote above all else the material well-being of the body and of life, but are utterly silent about their spiritual welfare and the very serious duties which their profession as Christians enjoins upon them. They are not ashamed to conceal sometimes, as though with a veil, certain fundamental maxims of the Gospel, for fear lest otherwise the people refuse to hear and follow them. It will certainly be the part of prudence to proceed gradually in laying down the truth, when one has to do with men completely strangers to us and completely separated from God. "Before using the steel, let the wounds be felt with a light hand," as Gregory said (*Registr.* v. 44 (18) ad Joannem episcop.). But even this carefulness would sink to mere prudence of the flesh, were it proposed as the rule of constant and everyday action—all the more since such a method would seem not to hold in due account that Divine Grace which sustains the sacerdotal ministry and

which is given not only to those who exercise this ministry, but to all the faithful of Christ in order that our words and our action may find an entrance into their heart. Gregory did not at all understand this prudence, either in the preaching of the Gospel, or in the many wonderful works undertaken by him to relieve misery. He did constantly what the Apostles had done, for they, when they went out for the first time into the world to bring into it the name of Christ, repeated the saying: "We preach Christ crucified, a scandal for the Jews, a folly for the Gentiles" (1 Corinthians 1:23). If ever there was a time in which human prudence seemed to offer the only expedient for obtaining something in a world altogether unprepared to receive doctrines so new, so repugnant to human passions, so opposed to the civilization, then at its most flourishing period, of the Greeks and the Romans, that time was certainly the epoch of the preaching of the faith. But the Apostles disdained such prudence, because they understood well the precept of God: "It pleased God by the foolishness of our preaching to save them that believe" (1 Corinthians 1:21). And as it ever was, so it is today, this foolishness "to them that are saved, that is, to us, is the power of God" (1 Corinthians 1:18). The scandal of the Crucified will ever furnish us in the future, as it has done in the past, with the most potent of all weapons; now, as of yore, in that sign we shall find victory.

27. But, Venerable Brethren, this weapon will lose much of its efficacy or be altogether useless in the hands of men not accustomed to the interior life with Christ, not educated in the school of true and solid piety, not thoroughly inflamed with zeal for the glory of God and for the propagation of His kingdom. So keenly did Gregory feel this necessity that he used the greatest care in creating bishops and priests

animated by a great desire for the divine glory and for the true welfare of souls. And this was the intent he had before him in his book on the *Pastoral Rule*, wherein are gathered together the laws regulating the formation of the clergy and the government of bishops—laws most suitable not for his times only but for our own. Like an "Argus full of light," says his biographer, "he moved all round the eyes of his pastoral solicitude through all the extent of the world" (Joann. Diac., lib ii. c. 55), to discover and correct the failings and the negligence of the clergy. Nay, he trembled at the very thought that barbarism and immortality might obtain a footing in the life of the clergy, and he was deeply moved and gave himself no peace whenever he learned of some infraction of the disciplinary laws of the Church, and immediately administered admonition and correction, threatening canonical penalties on transgressors, sometimes immediately applying these penalties himself, and again removing the unworthy from their offices without delay and without human respect.

28. Moreover, he inculcated the maxims which we frequently find in his writings in such form as this: "In what frame of mind does one enter upon the office of mediator between God and man who is not conscious of being familiar with grace through a meritorious life?" (*Reg. Past.* i. 10). "If passion lives in his actions, with what presumption does he hasten to cure the wound, when he wears a scar on his very face?" (*Reg. Past.* i. 9). What fruit can be expected for the salvation of souls if the apostles "combat in their lives what they preach in their words?" (*Reg. Past.* i. 2). "Truly he cannot remove the delinquencies of others who is himself ravaged by the same" (*Reg. Past.* i. 11).

29. The picture of the true priest, as Gregory understands and describes him, is the man "who, dying to all passions of the flesh, already lives spiritually; who has no thought for the prosperity of the world; who has no fear of adversity; who desires only internal things; who does not permit himself to desire what belongs to others but is liberal of his own; who is all bowels of compassion and inclines to forgiveness, but in forgiveness never swerves unduly from the perfection of righteousness; who never commits unlawful actions, but deplores as though they were his own the unlawful actions of others; who with all affection of the heart compassionates the weakness of others, and rejoices in the prosperity of his neighbor as in his own profit; who in all his doings so renders himself a model for others as to have nothing whereof to be ashamed, at least, as regards his external actions; who studies so to live that he may be able to water the parched hearts of his neighbors with the waters of doctrine; who knows through the use of prayer and through his own experience that he can obtain from the Lord what he asks" (*Reg. Past.* i. 10).

30. How much thought, therefore, Venerable Brethren, must the Bishop seriously take with himself, and in the presence of God, before laying hands on young levites! "Let him never dare, either as an act of favor to anybody, or in response to petitions made to him, to promote any one to sacred orders whose life and actions do not furnish a guarantee of worthiness" (*Registr.* v 63 (58) ad universos episcopos per Hellad.). With what deliberation should he reflect before entrusting the work of the apostolate to newly ordained priests! If they be not duly tried under the vigilant guardianship of more prudent priests, if there be not abundant evidence of their morality, of their inclination for

spiritual exercises, of their prompt obedience to all the norms of action which are suggested by ecclesiastical custom or proved by long experience, or imposed by those whom "the Holy Ghost has placed as bishops to rule the Church of God" (Acts 20:28), they will exercise the sacerdotal ministry not for the salvation but for the ruin of the Christian people. For they will provoke discord, and excite rebellion, more or less tacit, thus offering to the world the sad spectacle of something like division amongst us, whereas in truth these deplorable incidents are but the pride and unruliness of a few. Oh! Let those who stir up discord be altogether removed from every office. Of such apostles the Church has no need; they are not apostles of Jesus Christ Crucified but of themselves.

31. We seem to see still present before Our eyes the Holy Pontiff Gregory at the Lateran Council, surrounded by a great number of bishops from all parts of the world. Oh, how fruitful is the exhortation that falls from his lips on the duties of the clergy! How his heart is consumed with zeal! His words are as lightnings rending the perverse, as scourges striking the indolent, as flames of divine love gently enfolding the most fervent. Read that wonderful homily of Gregory, Venerable Brethren, and have it read and meditated by your clergy, especially during the annual retreat (Hom. in Evang. i. 17).

32. Among other things, with unspeakable sorrow he exclaims: "Lo, the world is full of priests, but rare indeed it is to find a worker in the hands of God; we do indeed assume the priestly office, but the obligation of the office we do not fulfill" (Hom. in Evang. n. 3). What force the Church would

have today could she count a worker in every priest! What abundant fruit would the supernatural life of the Church produce in souls were it efficaciously promoted by all. Gregory succeeded in his own times in strenuously stimulating this spirit of energetic action, and such was the impulse given by him that the same spirit was kept alive during the succeeding ages. The whole mediaeval period bears what may be called the Gregorian imprint; almost everything it had indeed came to it from the Pontiff—the rule of ecclesiastical government, the manifold phases of charity and philanthropy in its social institutions, the principles of the most perfect Christian asceticism and of monastic life, the arrangement of the liturgy and the art of sacred music.

33. The times are indeed greatly changed. But, as We have more than once repeated, nothing is changed in the life of the Church. From her Divine Founder she has inherited the virtue of being able to supply at all times, however much they may differ, all that is required not only for the spiritual welfare of souls, which is the direct object of her mission, but also everything that aids progress in true civilization, for this follows as a natural consequence of that same mission.

34. For it cannot be but that the truths of the supernatural order, of which the Church is the depository, promote also everything that is true, good, and beautiful in the order of nature, and this the more efficaciously in proportion as these truths are traced to the supreme principle of all truth, goodness and beauty, which is God.

35. Human science gains greatly from revelation, for the latter opens out new horizons and makes known sooner other truths of the natural order, and because it opens the true road to investigation and keeps it safe from errors of application and of method. Thus does the lighthouse show many things they otherwise would not see, while it points out the rocks on which the vessel would suffer shipwreck.

36. And since, for our moral discipline, the Divine Redeemer proposes as our supreme model of perfection His heavenly Father (Matthew v. 48), that is, the Divine goodness itself, who can fail to see the mighty impulse thence accruing to the ever more perfect observance of the natural law inscribed in our hearts, and consequently to the greater welfare of the individual, the family, and universal society? The ferocity of the barbarians was thus transformed to gentleness, woman was freed from subjection, slavery was repressed, order was restored in the due and reciprocal independence upon one another of the various classes of society, justice was recognized, the true liberty of souls was proclaimed, and social and domestic peace assured.

37. Finally, the arts modeled on the supreme exemplar of all beauty which is God Himself, from whom is derived all the beauty to be found in nature, are more securely withdrawn from vulgar concepts and more efficaciously rise towards the ideal, which is the life of all art. And how fruitful of good has been the principle of employing them in the service of divine worship and of offering to the Lord everything that is deemed to be worthy of him, by reason of its richness, its goodness, its elegance of form. This principle has created

sacred art, which became and still continues to be the foundation of all profane art. We have recently touched upon this in a special motu proprio, when speaking of the restoration of the Roman Chant according to the ancient tradition and of sacred music. And the same rules are applicable to the other arts, each in its own sphere, so that what has been said of the Chant may also be said of painting, sculpture, architecture; and towards all these most noble creations of genius the Church has been lavish of inspiration and encouragement. The whole human race, fed on this sublime ideal, raises magnificent temples, and here in the House of God, as in its own house, lifts up its heart to heavenly things in the midst of the treasures of all beautiful art, with the majesty of liturgical ceremony, and to the accompaniment of the sweetest of song.

38. All these benefits, We repeat, the action of the Pontiff St. Gregory succeeded in attaining in his own time and in the centuries that followed; and these, too, it will be possible to attain today, by virtue of the intrinsic efficacy of the principles which should guide us and of the means we have at our disposal, while preserving with all zeal the good which by the grace of God is still left us and "restoring in Christ" (Ephesians 1:10) all that has unfortunately lapsed from the right rule.

39. We are glad to be able to close these Our Letters with the very words with which St. Gregory concluded his memorable exhortation in the Lateran Council: "These things, Brethren, you should meditate with all solicitude yourselves and at the same time propose for the meditation of your neighbor.

Prepare to restore to God the fruit of the ministry you have received. But everything we have indicated for you we shall obtain much better by prayer than by our discourse. Let us pray: O God, by whose will we have been called as pastors among the people, grant, we beseech Thee, that we may enabled to be in Thy sight what we are said to be by the mouths of men" (*Hom. cit.,* ii. 18).

40. And while We trust by the intercession of the holy Pontiff Gregory that God may graciously hear Our prayer, We impart to all of you, Venerable Brethren, and to your clergy and people, the Apostolic benediction with all the affection of Our heart, as a pledge of heavenly favors and in token of Our paternal good will.

Given at Rome at St. Peter's on March 12, of the year 1904, on the feast of St. Gregory I. Pope and Doctor of the Church, in the first year of Our Pontificate.

PIUS X, POPE

Made in the USA
Middletown, DE
22 August 2019